Trust Your Journey
PRAYER JOURNAL

with inpiring prayers from Pastor Barbara Palmer,
lead intercessor at Kingdom Celebration Center.

Barbara Palmer

TRUST YOUR JOURNEY PRAYER JOURNAL

Copyright ©2021 by Barbara Palmer

All rights reserved. No portion of this book can be reproduced, stored in a retrieval system, or transmitted in any form or by any means—electronic, mechanical, photocopy, recording, scanning, or other—except for brief quotations in critical reviews or articles, without the prior written permission of the publisher.

Published by Kingdom Publishing, LLC
Odenton, Maryland 21113
United States of America

Unless otherwise noted, Scripture quotations are taken from King James Version (marked KJV), public domain. Scriptures marked ESV are taken from THE HOLY BIBLE, ENGLISH STANDARD VERSION (ESV): Scriptures taken from THE HOLY BIBLE, ENGLISH STANDARD VERSION® Copyright© 2001 by Crossway, a publishing ministry of Good News Publishers. Used by permission. Scripture marked CJB are taken from the COMPLETE JEWISH BIBLE (CJB): Scripture taken from the COMPLETE JEWISH BIBLE, copyright© 1998 by David H. Stern. Published by Jewish New Testament Publications, Inc. www.messianicjewish.net/jntp. Distributed by Messianic JEwish Resources Int'l. www.messianicjewish.net. All rights reserved. Used by permission.

ISBN 978-1-947741-63-8

Edited by Mary Perara

Cover Design by Antonio Palmer

INTRODUCTION

I birthed this prayer book out of my private time with Daddy God. There were mornings He would wake me and tell me to go downstairs to pray for certain people. Then He would say, "Send them this prayer." As I began to write out of a place of obedience, I did not understand how the things God shared with me would be the answer to someone's request to Him.

Several people suggested I add these prayers in a book as a reflection of what Adonai said to them at the moment.

As you read this book of prayers, it is my hope that the anointing of the Holy Spirit will cause walls to fall and burdens to be removed over you (to include any situation you are walking through). It is my heart for you not only to read these prayers, but for you to use the space provided to pour out your heart to the father with your own prayers.

"Father, Daddy, Adonai, Jehovah, Roi, Elyon, Nissi, Rapha, we thank You for blessing us with Your ever-present love. We adore You for Your grace and mercy, and lovingkindness that continues to draw us closer to You. We yearn for Your voice to speak to us, and we yearn for Your return. Eyes have not seen, and ears have not heard; neither has it entered the hearts of man the things You have prepared for us because we love You.

When we read what You are ministering to us through these prayers, remember Your promises and answer according to Your purpose for us, In Jesus Name, amen."

Lovingly,

Barbara Palmer

Your daughter (the one who cries out to You)
Barbara - the foreigner, the stranger, the one who is just passing through!

CONTENTS

Communion 8

Praise 10

Purpose 14

Commitment 18

Praise 20

Gratefulness 24

Thanksgiving 26

Exaltation 28

Submission 30

Healing 32

Women in Leadership 34

Fasting 36

Visitation 38

Covering 42

Relationship 46

Business Ventures 50

Victory 52

Assignment	54
Newness	56
Friendship	58
Renewal	62
Mindset	64
Encouragement	66
Vulnerability	68
Humility	70
Grace	72
Alignment	74
Supplication	78
Surrender	80
Deeper	82
Confidence	84
Adoration	86
Revelation	88
Invitation	90
Sustainability	92
Intercession for Leaders	94

Persecution 98

Petition 100

Exchange 104

Intercession for Prayer Warriors 106

Presence 108

Desire 110

Breakthrough 112

Cleansing 114

Faith 116

Exhortation 120

Expectation 124

Awakening 126

Obedience 130

Deliverance 134

Increase 136

Lovingkindness 138

Communion

"Father, I pray for Your lovingkindness and tender mercies to saturate me. Daddy, I cast my crown down before You in worship today. All of who I am becomes dim when I worship You. When You walk into the room, I strip myself of all that I desire and have achieved, to include my degrees and titles. In my time with You, I share Your glory with no one, as I bear my thoughts before You now. God, Your train fills the temple and Your glory hovers over Your entrance. All demonic activity fails when You arrive. I evade all tactics and plots. Your presence is all I need today.

Come in and sup with us, Daddy. We need Your glory like never before! Break mindsets, change thought patterns and renew us today. Heart Fixer, fix us today. Awesome Deliverer, deliver us today, and restructure our very being. King Jesus, when You walk in, all our questions, concerns, and problems become dim. We need You to break our traditions and make us new! Fix our marriages, mend broken hearts and heal families. Cause judgements and lawsuits to be trampled under our feet! Comfort those who are without income today. Make a way for those who are unemployed. Give them minds to create their own business.

God, heal those that are sick as Your presence fills the room. Bring people back to their right minds. Release vision and creativity. Daddy, loose shackles and birth today! Our prayer is for joy to be restored. Daddy, cause us to win souls that are lost and not those that just come to church. God, we are failing You as a nation and as a people! Daddy, walk in Congress and in the White House. Walk in our churches, in our homes and in our jobs today.

We give You free reign Daddy and bow before You. Cause us to stop what we are doing and acknowledge You as You walk in the room. Thank You Father, for gifting us with Your presence, and thank You for taking Your seat on the throne of our hearts. In Jesus Name, amen and amen!"

Trust Your Journey - Share Your Thoughts

Promise

"Father, I rejoice in knowing that Your eyes saw my unformed substance and decided to make me fearfully and wonderfully in Your sight. O Lord, You have searched me and known me. You know when I lie down and when I rise, and You discern my thoughts from afar. You search out my path and You're acquainted with all my ways. Even before a word is on my tongue, behold, O Lord, You know me. Search me, O God, and know my heart! Try me and know my thoughts. See if there are any grievous ways in me and lead me in the way everlasting!

As we rise, our hearts desire each day is to represent You well as citizens of Your kingdom. When all things fail around us, one thing remains true… and that is YOU! Lord, we know Your desire for Your children is to cast all our cares upon You, for You care for us. As we are placed in this world, we recognize today that we are just foreigners on a journey to our promise, and we anticipate reigning with You.

Call Your people from all parts of the earth. Speak to us God, cause us to rise and take our positions of authority so You can be lifted, as we are drawn to You. Let us not become weary in well doing; for in due season we shall reap if we faint not! As we lay ourselves upon You, please don't forget Your promises towards us. You promised never to leave us nor forsake us, and that You would never see the righteous forsaken, nor our seed begging bread. You said that all Your promises are yes and amen.

Lord, you stated that if we are faithful and obedient, we would eat the good of the land. Your Word says that You would give Your angels charge over us to keep us! It also says if we have faith as the grain of a mustard seed and not doubt as we ask, then You shall bring it to pass. Also, if we bring our tithe into the storehouse, You would open the windows of heaven and pour us out a blessing that we would not have room to receive. You declared You would withhold no good thing from those who walk upright before You.

We are declaring, speaking and reminding You of Your Word today. Your promises said we would be the head and not the tail, and that we would be blessed coming in and going out. If I give, it shall be given unto me… pressed down, shaken together and running over, shall men give unto my bosom.

Lord, You promise that no weapon formed against us shall prosper, and every tongue that rises against us in judgment shall be condemned! You promised I would be above and not beneath, and when the enemy comes in like a flood, Your spirit will raise up a standard against it. Most of all Your promise to me is eternal life, and that I would prosper and be in good health even as my soul prospers! We remember Your promises today, declare them from the rooftop this morning, and stand in agreement with Your word. It is so!"

Trust Your Journey - Share Your Thoughts

Trust Your Journey - Share Your Thoughts

Purpose

"Father, I thank You for purpose. I thank You that Your Son was chosen before the foundation of the world was laid. Thank You for creating us in Your heavenly workshop, and instilling in us all things we would need to walk in our divine assignment and purpose. Each test we have encountered, each blessing we received, and every mistake we've made only makes us want to please You even more. Our worship is authentic because we know what it took to reach key milestones in our lives.

Daddy, teach us to walk in our assignments without malicious thoughts or unforgiveness. Teach us to endure our trials as a good soldier and to walk in love as You did. Our purpose is to re-pre-sent You on the earth. Father, as we move forward today in our purpose, let us be aware of what we take in and what we give out. Remind us to pray for those who are weak and love on those who are broke. Let us rejoice with those who guide us to speak of You wherever we go. Help us Father to become Your mirror so that when people see us, they see a reflection of You.

Daddy, You are seeking those who want to worship You in spirit and in truth. As we seek You out this morning, let our yes be real, our amen be sincere and let our choices in life please You. Adonai, when we mess up (and we will), teach us to remain humble and to repent for our wrongdoings so You can come in and commune with us. Come meet our needs and satisfy our thirst for more of You. We are heirs and joint heirs with Christ, and partakers of Your nature.

Father, speak to us, open doors for us and extend a heart for prayer to people concerning us. God, place us on their minds and cause them to sow into Your children. The wealth of the wicked is laid up for the just. We pray for the release of necessary resources to handle Your affairs well. We also lift up prayers that doors will sling wide open, and we desire to meet the needs of each person. May blessings come forth and be granted for the following petitions:

New jobs
New visions
Children being restored back to You
Job reassignments

Dreams
Ministries activated
Families restored
Marriages revived
Churches growing with new members
Bodies healed
Bank account replenished
Cars repaired
New homes
Deliverance

God, we say come today with power and strength for Your people. There is greatness and abundance You have prepared for us that love You. Show up Daddy, rise from Your majestic throne and come see about us. Yes, You can send angels as well as people; but there are times we need You to come and remind us You are Rapha; You are Elyon and Nissi! We await Your arrival and anticipate what You want to say to us. Blow the trumpet and sound the alarm King of Kings, for You are in the Holy temple. Let all the earth discern when to be silent and listen for Your sound. Amen and amen! It is so!"

Trust Your Journey - Share Your Thoughts

Trust Your Journey - Share Your Thoughts

Commitment

"I Love You, Father! We trust daily that You are doing exceedingly and abundantly above all we can ask or think in our lives; according to Your infinite power. You've deposited Your spiritual DNA in us so we would have all that we need to walk in our destiny and purpose. Our hearts cry for Your kingdom to come and Your will be done, on earth as it is in heaven. We speak over a sound mind, an overflow of Your Spirit, and an increase in wisdom and knowledge in Your word. We also speak that many souls will come to know You because we opened our mouths as an instrument for Your work.

We believe many lives will be transformed into Your kingdom because we decided to open our mouths and shout yes to You, anyway! We say yes to:

Reading Your word

Praying

Forgiving

Sacrifice

Humility

Repentance

Loving on those who persecute us and slander us

Feeding those who are hungry

Clothing the naked

Laying aside our pride so we can hear from You

We rent our garments, Lord as we go beyond the veil and enter the holy of holies. It is in that place that You require a broken and sincere heart. We are broken before You this morning and we declare You to be righteous.

Thank You Adonai, for capturing our very being, and for pulling us close to Your bosom. We know You are the Most High God. At Your Name, demons flee, and we tremble. By Your name, the sick are healed and lives go from broken to victory! Your Name, Lord is a strong tower where the righteous run in and they are safe. You set order wherever You go. You said let there be and there was! You said come forth, and we did; be filled, and we were! How marvelous are Your works! Glory to God!"

Trust Your Journey - Share Your Thoughts

Praise

"Good Morning Daddy! We honor and celebrate You today for being our Way Maker, Deliverer, Sounding Board, Chief Problem Solver and Advocate! We so love on You Father for sustained life and complete health. We thank You because You have confidence in us as Your children to accomplish great things. We follow hard after Your promises Lord; for there are many and they are great. Thank You for making sure that our equilibrium remains on balance and that You calibrate every part of our being. We are fearfully and wonderfully made! No matter where we go or what we do, Your presence is always abiding inside of us!

God, we thank You for assigning Angels that move to and fro the earth with the promises and command that You have set forth in our lives. The enemy has a plan, but Your plan for us is covered under Your wings! Your blood is priceless, and Your Name is great! We shall rejoice and speak out Your word daily so we will not sin against You! Thank You Lord for granting us wholeness, soundness of mind and healed bodies! You call our families blessed, and we are honored that all our needs will be met according to Your riches in glory.

We stand in agreement Lord, as Your children knowing that all Your promises are yes and amen! We don't take You for granted Daddy, for we are thankful of all things. When our minds become interrupted by the cares of life, we remain steadfast and unmovable; always abiding in You!

We praise You today Great Provider, All-Knowing and Ever-Present God! Your people will shout with a voice of triumph and give no room for the devil to steal our praise today. You are El Roi (the God who sees), and El Shaddai (the God almighty)! You are El Elyon (the Most High God), and Yahweh (our Lord)! Father, you are Elohim (our God), Jehovah Nissi (our Banner) and Jehovah Rapha (the one who heals us)! Yes Lord, Your Names have great meaning to Your people!

You are Abba, our Father! You are Jesus our soon coming King! From everlasting to everlasting, Your Name shall be praised! We stand before You as exposed beings; knowing that all You see before us is our vulnerability! We rise today knowing that You will perform miracles, signs and wonders according to Your power that is released over us!

Come Lord, come like You promised. Meet, fulfill and sustain all our needs. Fill our spirits with songs of praise, as our mouths open to utter this prayer or praise of thanksgiving, in Jesus Name!"

Trust Your Journey - Share Your Thoughts

Trust Your Journey - Share Your Thoughts

Gratefulness

"Daddy, Adonai, All-Knowing and Ever-Present God. We extend ourselves to You this morning with a grateful heart and release our praise to You this day. Our mind is sensitive to how You made our earthly bodies, and You breathe the breath of life into each of us! We kneel before You in total adoration. Daddy, there is none like You, and You shall reign on earth forevermore! We summoned our angels to be on post today and deliver the rewards and spoils that You have laid up for us. Our praise will capture Your attention and Your heart. Thank You for being jealous over us! Jeremiah 29:12 teaches us that when we call upon You and pray, You will hearken unto us.

God, we bless Your Holy Name and thank You for such a privilege to wake us this morning. As we enter Your gates with thanksgiving and Your courts with praise, we are so thankful and grateful for this day. Cause us to turn to Your Word; for we know when things fail, the power of Your Word remains. There is so much hidden in Your Word that can cause us to feel overwhelmed at times, but necessary all the time. We find ourselves in Your book, which is right where we need to be. Love on us today Daddy as we love on You. We are so desperate for You and yearn to go deeper. We desire to go higher in our time with You. Come Lord, come Abba, Yahweh, and El Shaddai, the Almighty. Jesus, from everlasting to everlasting, Your Name shall be proclaimed!"

Trust Your Journey - Share Your Thoughts

Thanksgiving

"Father in the Name of Jesus, we rejoice in You for allowing us to open our eyes today to see Your great creation! Thank You for giving us ears to hear and the utilization of our limbs; to rise out of bed and walk around. We are thankful for the ability to breathe fresh air, and our use of sight to view all the wonderful colors You've made. Lord, we're overjoyed that our family members are here with us, and we're grateful for the gift of another day to tell them we love them.

We thank You for our church home and the body of believers we fellowship with weekly, who have become our spiritual family that we can embrace and fellowship with. We say glory to Your Name Father, for every blessing deposited to include our jobs, businesses, and careers. You ordained our gifts and allowed us to flourish knowing we would intentionally represent You well. We are most grateful that those careers have opened doors for us to purchase a lovely home and car(s). Thank You, God that we can sow into Your kingdom for such a time as this. Sometimes Daddy we forget to say thank You for these blessings. Lord, we take them for granted because of our skills and missteps caused by rushed activities.

You are our King, and we pause for a selah moment just to praise You. Your word states to let everything that has breath praise the Lord. We praise You Daddy in all things. Our praise is our weapon of warfare, and it is also an indicator to the enemy that we are awake and ready for our daily assignment. Our praise confuses, baffles, and angers the enemy. So today we praise! We praise You, God past our yesterday, any hurts beyond what we see, and all throughout the day."

Trust Your Journey - Share Your Thoughts

Exaltation

"Oh, magnify the Lord with me saints and let us exalt His Name together! He hears our praises and will rise from His throne to marvel at the sound! Praise come forth this day! Praise, revive this moment and let it drown out our daily thoughts! Let our praise bring us into destiny and an overflow in the Spirit! Let praise arise in this gathering and anticipate Your move! Needs are met when we praise. Praise! Praise! Praise!

Father, we rest at Your feet today. We come open and vulnerable; humbling ourselves at Your throne. We recognize that we have not moved in our purpose on our own accord. Your presence and a touch of grace are the ingredients to a fulfilling life. It is beyond measure that we can call upon You and gain an audience with You, our King! Lord, Your desire is for us to come and pray to You. As You incline Your ear to our voice, You long to see what we pour out in Your presence.

Let us taste and see that You are good, for we know that it pleases You to bless Your children. Fill us again, Lord with Your mighty power and we shall be made whole! Your presence brings such peace and assurance that You are with us; You are faithful and just. Never forget our heart to serve the kingdom! Arrest our minds, will, and emotions; challenge us to become more like You each day! We say Abba; You are welcome here! As we stand under an open heaven, pour out spiritual revelation, open doors and deposit increase in all areas of our lives! We love You today, Daddy and we say amen and amen!"

Trust Your Journey - Share Your Thoughts

Submission

"Father, we stand in awe of who You are. Thank You for the crushing and the bruising moments that have created a place of intimacy with You. You are our Father and You desire good things for Your children. As we realign ourselves with Your purpose, we say thank You for loving us unconditionally. Thank You for covering our families, jobs and our health.

Thank You God, for giving Your angels charge over us and for keeping us from seen and unseen danger. You remain faithful to us even when we fall! Father, our desire and cry is to always please You. We know by pleasing You, we shall experience some bruising, but will remain steadfast in our faith walk with You. As trials come into our lives, we MUST remain faithful.

God, create in us a clean heart and renew a right spirit within us so we will remember our identity and purpose! Birth all of who you are in us daily Lord! Surround us with Your goodness as we cry unto You with our whole hearts. Deep is now calling into deep! Speak! Speak Lord! We place our ears back to the doorpost of Your heart so we can hear Your desires concerning us and Your church! Come Lord like You promised. Your servants avail themselves to hear what You want to say! Speak!"

Trust Your Journey - Share Your Thoughts

Healing

"Thank You, Adonai for caring for us as only You can. Father, we rejoice in You today for Your faithfulness, lovingkindness and tender mercies that are new daily! Great is thy faithfulness! Thank You so much for divine healing and complete restoration. Lord, cover all those that need Your healing power, and help them push past their trials to reach You! Thank You Jesus that all things will be provided for us on our behalf. Thank You for speaking to us during these moments to position people when and where they're needed.

May each financial and attendance goals be met through every door You have opened for ministry. All who attend strategic times with you in various conferences and meetings will walk out the doors free and confident to walk in their purpose. Place a hedge around all leaders Lord with Your shield of protection, provision and wisdom. In Jesus Name, amen and amen!"

Trust Your Journey - Share Your Thoughts

Women in Leadership

"Father, we adore You this morning oh God! We are Your children and are seated in heavenly places. We take our seat of authority and come with an expectancy this morning. You are faithful toward us and we adore You for Your devotion. You know the plans You have towards us and they are truly for our good! Thank You for making countless ways out of no way, for meeting every need and hearing every request! We speak life to all our situations today and we call forth those things that are not as though they are, in Jesus Name.

Father, thank You for women of God everywhere, and Your vision to help them grow in You. For the leader You have put in place to reach others; give her the strength to see You and hear Your voice when You pour into her thoughts! Open her mind to bring women together to hear You speak. I pray that she will remain faithful in believing that many women will gather at her events to spend time with You.

Lord, I pray for an increase in registrations to be above and beyond what the conduit of Your Word sees. I pray for the support of other leaders to encourage other women to register. May women attend spiritual empowerment conferences from each state, particularly the DC, Maryland and Virginia (DMV) area. God, let this gathering reach a multitude that need to hear from you. Pour Your wisdom into Your servant Lord, to increase her confidence to walk in her calling. I pray strength and endurance through any attack that comes her way! Father, may she remain steadfast and unmovable… always abounding in her purpose. We bless You for this Woman of God, cover her in prayer, and may Your banner wrap her in love and peace today, in Jesus Name!"

Trust Your Journey - Share Your Thoughts

Fasting

"Father, I adore You this morning for Your lovingkindness and tender mercies. You desire truth in all we say and do. We bring forth fruit that is necessary for repentance; according to Matthew3:8. We offer ourselves as a living sacrifice, holy and acceptable which is our reasonable service. We clothe ourselves with repentance as we prepare for our time of fasting with You. It is a fast that You have called; the one that commands us to decrease so You can increase in us. This fast tears down our strongholds internally so you can use us mightily!

Create in us a clean heart oh God, and renew the right spirit within us. As people come through our doors, we can assist their needs and lead them directly to You. We understand that it is because of Your grace that You visit us. You are our great King and You desire Your citizens to represent You well. Today, we yield to the revival process and submit our bodies as a living sacrifice. You are commanding us to become the sacrifice in this hour so Your glory can be revealed.

God, place a shield of protection around our children, homes and finances so we can continue to strive in excellence as You lead us! We shall proclaim Your Name upon this earth and shout it from the rooftops! You, oh Lord are returning to Your glorious church that is without spot or wrinkle. Thank You for correcting us, challenging us and slaying our inner mindset so we can be that church.

Father, thank You for Your hand that accompanies Your presence and always reminds us You are near! Great miracles shall be bought forth in this hour, and Your desire is to use us for Your kingdom. Make us ready Lord and smite the things within us that displease You! Come Holy Spirit and visit us today to bring forth tangible fruit needed to birth Your plan in us! God visit us! Please visit us! We need to hear Your voice in this hour! It is not by might, nor by power; but Your Spirit that we can stand before You on this day! We love You so much and we're so thankful for You! Amen and amen!"

Trust Your Journey - Share Your Thoughts

Visitation

"Lord, Your children are so grateful for the consistency of Your visitation. We are thankful that You have decided to visit us in a way that is refreshing and deliberate. God, we have done nothing to deserve or merit this moment with You. You always choose a people, a place, and a time to release Your Spirit! Father, You have been hovering over the earth with an open door to those that would let You in! Your presence is so strong upon the face of the earth that it causes volcanos to erupt, storms to shout and wind or rain to be directed at Your command! There's strength in Your presence that causes people to run freely to Your house for deliverance, and with love and forgiveness in their hearts like never before!

Father, Your desire for us runs deep! Thank You for allowing our hearts to experience You! Thank You for rest and for pouring out Your Spirit! Cause an awakening in us and in those around us! Release you signs and wonders and set people free from lifestyles that don't please You. Deliver people from addictions that have kept them bound for years and transform mindsets over night! We are in a season of craving Your tangible presence.

Thank You for the angels who have charge over us to keep us in all our ways. Cause them to work on our behalf and on the behalf of Your kingdom! Your will is done in this hour! Confuse and confound the enemy when he attempts to attach himself to Your children. Give us strategic intel on how to fight the devil during this hour. We so appreciate Your voice and Your grace that showers over us! Speak today Holy Spirit! We cannot survive without You or exist without Your Word! Speak a word that will transform us into better citizens of Your kingdom, for our desire is to please our king! Glory!

In this hour, You are looking for those of us who want more of You. We can sense it and feel Your presence! Have Your way Jesus! Your people who desire You will receive You! Invade, abide and captivate us! Come in like a mighty rushing wind! Place Your finger on our hearts until we are tender enough to sense Your presence! Move Holy Spirit, move! We declare victory today and will walk in complete confidence in all Your decisions over our lives! Thanks Daddy for Your power that works within us!"

Trust Your Journey - Share Your Thoughts

Trust Your Journey - Share Your Thoughts

Covering

"Father, I magnify You this morning for Your Omnipresence. You are the one and only God that truly cares about Your people, and You love us well. Even when we don't see what direction You are taking us, You scoop us up in the palm of Your hands and lead us in a plain path. Father, You resuscitate us from apparent death! Resuscitate can sometimes places us in the ICU until we gain strength and clarity. We may even be a little weak, but that is when You become strong within us!

Lord, You know what each of us need in this hour. We don't have to fight each other to determine who will lie in Your bosom first, for You can feed all of us at the same time. The nourishment that You provide is life-giving, and it sustains us through each season. You are causing the whole earth to travail in this hour. One of Your heart's desires is for Your children to be prepared for the greatest revival that will ever occur upon the face of the earth! This revival will prove to many that You are the one and only true Living God!

Jesus, we stand in awe of You today! What You want to do in us is so great, that we must yield and give way to Your purpose! Don't let us miss Your hour of visitation, for it is here! We petition You to open our ears to hear You speak! Speak as we sleep, when we awake, while we are at work, in our car or in the store.

Lord wherever we go, speak. Your servant is ready to hear and will not place the wisdom You provide in a box. However You desire to speak Father, we avail ourselves to You. Not our will, but Yours be done! Come swiftly as we crucify our flesh and speak to us concerning us! We don't look at man in this hour; we look inward and ask that You transform us! We want to be good representatives of Your kingdom. Your heart longs for us to reside in Your kingdom and to learn to place our flesh under subjection to Your Holy Spirit!

God, You are such a good Father that even when we don't know what we need or what to pray; You make intercession on our behalf! Thank You so much for the angels You have given charge over us! Release them to surround us, fight for us, speak to us and care for us. Make us sensitive enough to know that they assist You in ensuring we do not stumble.

Father when our foes come against us, we know You will fight on our behalf! Protect and guard us from every fiery dart of the wicked one! God, we desire to see You perform miracles today! Show us Your glory! Cause Your face to shine upon us and we will be made whole. Now let the words of our mouth and the meditation of our hearts be acceptable in Your sight, oh Lord our Resuscitator and Redeemer!

"I give thanks to ADONAI with all my heart. I will tell about all Your wonderful deeds. I will be glad and exult in You. I will sing praise to Your Name, Elyon." Tehillim (Psa) 9:2-3 CJB"

Trust Your Journey - Share Your Thoughts

Trust Your Journey - Share Your Thoughts

Relationship

"Father, I thank You for my enduring friendships and the call that is on their lives to do Your will! Thank You for their diligence and persistence to allow You to birth what You desire in this hour. I stand in agreement that You will get the glory; and may the shackles be broken, and wounds healed over every woman You are connected to, in Jesus Name. Women follow other women who are confident in not only who they are, but what You have called them to.

Thank You God that my friends in the ministry have a deep relationship with You! Continue to love on them, support them and enlarge their heart for everyone they meet because their need to care and encourage others is so great.

Your wind is blowing toward my dear friends in this season, and I value and appreciate their obedience to hear Your voice! Daddy, You are such a loving and compassionate Father, a Care Giver and Provider. I petition You on their behalf to meet every need, answer every prayer, and move in their direction. Cover my friend's families, children, finances and their mind. Keep them healthy; for we are wise to the tricks of the enemy! You know the heart for us is to love others. When we allow individuals into our space, we don't take lightly the value of connections.

When tribulations arise, remind my friends that Your arms are wrapped around them tight. What the devil meant for evil will be utilized for Your perfect will. These Women of God have considered the cost and still said yes! Oh Father, I cry out to you; for what concerns them, also concerns me! What bothers them, bothers me! Thank You for finding me worthy to carry the burden of intercession for them.

God, bring every prophetic word to pass as this year is significant for their call! It is my honor to lay myself aside to keep my friends lifted, and I recognize that my time with You is precious when it involves praying for them.

Remove stressful people from their lives! There are Pastor's Wives who want to commit suicide, or want to check into a mental institution. They're fighting the urge to backslide, but You oh God have dispatched a multitude of Pastor's Wives to rescue these women! They are women in authority; yet they still know how to be under authority. Thank You for covering the Women of God and for keeping her humble and faithful. All the ways You want to pour into them, we ask that you do it Father. Speak Lord, for Your servant not only hears but will obey! In Jesus Name, amen!"

Trust Your Journey - Share Your Thoughts

Trust Your Journey - Share Your Thoughts

Business Ventures

"May each person who purchased your book today be liberated by every word. May every person reading your book never feel alone, hurt, broken, misunderstood, or rejected again because of the encouraging words you shared. They will know that they are supported, called and chosen by the King to be strengthened and honored! Every fiery dart of the wicked one must be demolished and crushed under your feet because you obeyed the Father's voice.

I declare that every women of God who cried and prayed (as I did) for someone to enter my life who understood my role and position, will find peace of mind; and that the Father will draw her to your book release, in Jesus Name! May word of your book spread to all corners of our nation, and pull out women everywhere who need your book! Life will arise in them from your obedience. I pray He rewards Your faithfulness with unmeasurable healing, in Jesus Name. I pray a hedge of protection surrounds you during your next level of calling while serving the Master.

The Lord promised that He will never leave nor forsake you, and He always keeps His promises concerning you! How much longer you ask before your promises are activated? Not long; it is right around the corner! One more push and it will be over, for you are crossing over into new joy! Yes, He ordained your book to be utilized to pull His daughter out of her trials and tests!

God has equipped you for this hour and has surrounded you with the right people to see this moment through. He loves you beyond measure, and will subdue and conquer your enemies. The Lord has so many blessings in store for you! Remain humble and at the feet of Jesus and watch how He moves for you in this season!"

Trust Your Journey - Share Your Thoughts

Victory

"Father, we rejoice in You today! You allowed us to wake up, breath in oxygen, open our eyes, and our mouths to give You praise. God, we have a voice that can be heard from the upper parts of each mountain, and down to the lowest parts where trouble awaits us. You have equipped us with an arsenal of weapons to fight every battle that is aimed our way! The enemy wants to sabotage every plan, purpose, gift, assignment, and well-being of Your people during our revival.

Jesus, we're so glad that You've not only exposed us to known attacks, but have taught us how to war against them. Our battle is never against flesh and blood, but against principalities and spiritual sickness in high places. We have Your Holy Spirit, and we have Your nature. Lord, You intentionally impregnated us with Your DNA when we were shaped into Your image.

God, we praise You and speak these declarations over ourselves today that we know who we are, and who we have in us... and it is You! We shall be whole and influential! We will be the righteousness of God, and walk in integrity! We will walk by faith and not by sight while proclaiming victory in You today! You have prepared great things for us and we are glad about it!

Thank You for strategy and for Your love! Come now Holy Spirit! Release all angels that are assigned to us and put them on assignment intentionally! Glory! I feel Your presence so strong this morning, and it speaks victory and revival! It speaks no disruptions on our jobs, our homes, our churches and even our minds! The weapons of warfare will form but they will crumble!

Jesus, we put the enemy on the run with Your Word today! You are our strong tower and You are concerned about us! You are King and You rule well! As Your children carry Your seed within us, we will rule well with You, and for You! Thank You for reminding us of who we are in You!"

Trust Your Journey - Share Your Thoughts

Assignment

"Jesus, You have graced us to abide on this earth, and we are partakers of Your divine nature. You have granted us access to all things that pertain to life and Godliness in Your kingdom. Grace us with the anointing to fulfill the assignment that You have given us; for we desire to walk worthy of the vocation You have assigned to us.

Lord, You are Alpha and Omega and have chosen us in this hour to live our purpose! Continue to give us wisdom on how to walk out this assignment as it pertains to our ministries, relationships and our marriages. Thank You for adding strength in our bodies and for unfailing health. Our mind, will and emotions will represent You well!

Lord, we are Your daughters who adore You. Keep our ears nailed to the doorpost of Your heart. We still desire to hear what You choose to speak through us. Thank You for resuscitating us and for jolting us back to You once again! We are grateful for all the angels that walk around us, cover us and bless us with peace. We face this day with an assurance that You are with us.

Although our adversary is lurking about, he has no authority over us because we are covered by the blood of Your dear Son, Jesus! When the enemy comes, it is only by permission You granted, because You know what we are made of and You know our assignment. God, we desire more of You. Thank You for revelation, for trusting us and for loving on us when we don't see or feel it. You are still yet nigh unto us and our hearts cry out to see You!

We are purposed to win many souls for You which calls for growth and development of Your citizens! Let the words of our mouth and the meditation of our hearts be acceptable to You our King! You are our strength and our redeemer! We will remain faithful to You in this season so we can reap the harvest! Come Holy Spirit come!"

Trust Your Journey - Share Your Thoughts

Newness

"Father we adore You for the fresh wind that is overtaking our church. We count it not robbery to rejoice in You! Your Name stays the same from everlasting to everlasting! We will shout from the very depths of our being that You are King! You take pleasure in blessing Your citizens and Your citizens take pleasure in adoring You! Jesus, we ask for Your supernatural powers to overtake and supersede our abilities today to produce results! We thrive because of Your loving kindness and tender mercies! Allow us to flourish not only in You, but in business, on our jobs and assignments.

Jesus, let the fruit of our lips always be of thanksgiving to You and Your people. Cause Your Face to shine upon us as we serve. All that we do, we want to re-pre-sent You well! Thank You for the open heaven opportunities You have given us. Now open our ears and provide creativity to our minds so we can grab the revelations for our lives, families, and churches from Your kingdom!

The highest honor we can give You, great King is not only our praise but our obedience in walking out our purpose. Your angels have been released and are now on assignment on our behalf! Thank You for the turning around our thoughts to match Yours. May doors swing wide open for miracles, signs and wonders to come through. We need outpourings to be released, shackles loosened and bondages broken, in Jesus Name! Fire consume us, and lovingkindness, overtake us. Anointing fall on us, for we are vulnerable in Your presence. Come, Lord come..."

Trust Your Journey - Share Your Thoughts

Friendship

"Father, thank You for the friends that are connected to every reader! Friendships are rare, precious and not to be taken lightly! Thank You for gracing us with the privilege to pray for them and the huge assignment You have placed on their lives. I thank You for their obedience to press even when they're attacked by the enemy! Take them to another level in You, Lord! I thank You that the greatness of friendships supersede our own individual victories! I thank You for divine connection and for revelation.

Lord, answer Your daughters today as we turn our faces towards You, and incline your voice to speak to us. You are calling forth friendships in this hour! Even when the uncertainties arise, we still say yes to our relationships! We encourage test and trials to turn for our friends! We speak life with these connections. Have Your way today, God! Bodies line up, minds line up and Spirit overtake us!

Father, we praise You for this day that You have created and give You glory. You said that we should rejoice in You always, and we do so with a cheerful heart. No matter what it looks like in the natural, our friendships will glorify You. In due season, we shall reap the joy of true relationship if we faint not. Touch our bodies and allow our minds to remember Your promises concerning us. Lord, we want Your very breath to hover over us today. We declare fresh winds to spring forth, and for the anointing to come and expand us! Winds of God come and hover over us! We call down Your presence in every situation today.

We open our hearts to allow You, Holy Spirit to bring back to our remembrance all the things You have taught us concerning friendships. Put a word in our mouth, place a song in our heart that will drive out all voices that are not Yours! We declare victory in You today. Meet every need and bring forth revelation. Lord, eyes have not seen and ears have not heard, and neither has it entered our hearts… the things You have prepared for those who love You. Be El-Elyon (God Most High) in our lives!

Jesus, may every captive thought regarding the encounter of our friendships surrender to You. We decree to remain committed to what You speak to us. Speak Lord; Your servants hear and obey! Rescue us from fear and doubt as You strengthen every friendship that represents You. If there are any friendships that are walking through various struggles; heal and restore these relationships right now Lord! We need one another according to Your plan! There is strength in numbers for Your kingdom. We are prepared to rise above our own thoughts to ensure Your guidance is deposited in our life accounts. Thank You Jesus for connecting Your people and we vow to never take these relationships for granted. In this season, we want Your will, in Jesus Name! Amen!"

Trust Your Journey - Share Your Thoughts

Trust Your Journey - Share Your Thoughts

Renewal

"Father, we adore You this morning and we honor You as King over our lives. You have established boundaries for Your citizen who reside in Your kingdom. So today, as we continue to hear from You, speak to us regarding the areas that exceed past our boundaries. You have placed a hedge around us for a reason, which includes protecting us from leaping into disobedience with our thoughts. Renew our mind God, so we can walk boldly into holiness with You. We repent for not understanding our duties and roles you have assigned to us. Your kingdom should represent You well; when we consider other avenues, we fall each time.

Lord, I pray that our words, attitudes and dispositions please You today. We know our steps are ordered by You. May we experience a great outpouring of Your Spirit like never before. We desire healing to take place at our church so that Your presence can be manifested in our city. Release the angels You have assigned to us to guard, protect, and ward off all evil threats in this hour. Speak to us about us! Speak to our minds regarding sickness and disease, health and wellness, selfcare, and our will and emotions. Your servants are listening. We've nailed our ears to Your heart! Speak Father, speak."

Trust Your Journey - Share Your Thoughts

Mindset

"Give ear to my words oh Lord, consider my meditation. Hearken into the voice of my cry, my King, for unto thee will I pray. My voice shall hear in the morning, for I will direct my prayer unto thee. Thou art not a God that hath pleasure in wickedness, neither shall evil dwell with thee. Father I thank You this day for Your faithfulness towards us Your people.

I thank You for being the head of Your people and the church. I take pleasure in the fact that I recognize my plans, ideas, and thoughts can never supersede the Holy Spirit and the direction You want to take us! Wreck us God in a way that will cause us to get out of our heads and into Your Word. The plans You have for us and our church are mission critical. No man knows the Father except he that is drawn to You. Draw us Lord! All our unrighteousness is nothing but filthy rags in Your sight.

Make us aware of our trespasses so we will not trespass against others. Shut our mouths from conversations that do not please You! Convict us when we enter into situations that do not concern us! If we are to continue living in revival, we must continue to repent daily. Repentance is simply changing our minds for the better! Help us lose the vision of negativity and see things more positively. Dismiss the spirit of finding fault, criticism and exchange it with compliments and goodness!

Turn our minds oh God! If I'm coming to You, I must have a distaste for my own ways! As an action agent, I am taking initiative to kill my old ways of thinking and replace them with Your thoughts! I want to have a "Metanoia" experience with You which means, beyond or outside of what my mind is accustomed to. I want a change of mind experience. You are trying to reach our minds!

Cause an illumination to take place in our thoughts that represent You. Transform our minds and let it be in us that is also in Christ Jesus! You desire our praise always, and You want our minds to remain fixed on You! Mind, we declare your obedience to the voice of God today. Mind, get out of God's way and line up with his will! May our minds seek the Lord, repent and rejoice Him! In Jesus Name, Amen!"

Trust Your Journey - Share Your Thoughts

Encouragement

"Father, I pray for all daughters everywhere tonight and ask that their thoughts line up to obey Your voice and not their plan. God, I pray that You will assure their tests will come to pass, and that You have greatness in store for them! The enemy's plan for their lives is to bypass their purpose, but we come against his tactics, in Jesus name. I pray they resist the sound of the enemy's voice when mistakes are made to try to tell our daughters they're not good enough. Jesus, help them remember that they are crown jewels in Your sight, and out of their pain will produce even greater purpose and anointing! Amen and amen!"

Trust Your Journey - Share Your Thoughts

Vulnerability

"Father, You told me to come boldly to the throne of grace! You want me to come to You without an attitude of entitlement. I live for You daily and move into the things You ask of me. Coming to You boldly means that I'm coming unreserved in my speech. My heart and mind is opened to You without arrogance, but with vulnerability. I know there is nothing in my thoughts that are hidden from You; for You are Omniscient.

Lord, today I will not attempt to cover up who I am in Your presence. All things are naked and exposed before You. You know my thoughts afar off, but You still take pleasure in me having an open and honest conversation about myself. Thank You for giving me Your ear so I can share every feeling and every moment with You. Wreck my inner self with Your lovingkindness, grace and Your mercy! If I expose my mind to anyone, it will be You!

Your Word can transcend time, space, and people; I take delight in that thought today! The enemy has a plan for my life. I will not complain or be concerned about those that have used, hurt or criticized me! I am a critic of myself in need of corrections. I know the plans You have for me will lead me to success! Strip away the old me, so that my heart is transparent before You. Amen!"

Trust Your Journey - Share Your Thoughts

Humility

"Father we come resting at Your feet as we prepare for the day. We humble ourselves at Your throne. Your children recognize that we have not gotten this far without You. Thank You for grace and mercy You have provided to us. It is beyond measure that we can call upon You and gain an audience with our King!

When we come to You God, we are blessed with quality time as we pour out our thoughts in Your presence. Fill us again Lord with Your mighty power, and we shall be made whole! Your presence brings such peace and assurance that You are with us!

Jesus, You are faithful and just; never forgetting what we do for the kingdom! Challenge us to become more like You each day! We say Abba; You are welcomed here today! As we stand under an open heaven, pour out spiritual revelation, open doors and bless us with increase in all areas of our lives! We love You Daddy, and we say amen and amen!"

Trust Your Journey - Share Your Thoughts

Grace

"Father, be our light today and shine in all that we say and do. As we push past our flesh to become the vessel You desire, let us come out of our cocoon and take in every breath You give us. For those who experienced tribulation in their last season, this season will require patience. Break forth God, and break walls. Your power is all together lovely and Your grace is sufficient. If we endure tribulation and invite in Your strength and power, we will inherit the promise.

Jesus, we thank You for whispering in our ears to not worry. Thank You for taking Your children by the hand and walking us from the outer courts, past the inner courts and into the holy of holies. It is a representation of just how much You love us. You are the only escort into the throne room. Father, help us take our time and not rush our thoughts in this room, because rushing can open the door to a false sense of humility and pride. Escorting us by hand allows You to take the lead and for us to follow!

Lord, we truly thank You for not giving us what we deserve, but choosing to pour Your love on Your children. Your covering is never designed to overwhelm or overtake us, but to fix and restore what we messed up. You want truth in the inwards parts of who we are, and the truth that is revealed from our time with You. As we enter Your presence, we are most thankful for You and bless Your holy name! Thank You for Psalms 10:12 and Psalms 10:17. Amen!"

Trust Your Journey - Share Your Thoughts

Alignment

"Father when You walk into a room, everything changes, and all things bow in Your presence. What seemed impossible now becomes possible. Prayers regarding tests that took weeks, months or years to fulfill will come to pass in seconds. If we stand in faith believing Your Word, it shall come to pass.

Your Word is hovering over us, brooding, and waiting on us to speak it by faith, so it can move. When our bodies, will and emotions line up to command blessings, Your Word shall move! Since we are heirs and joint heirs with Your son Jesus, all we must do is speak what we hear from You and it shall come to pass. This is the hour in which we must remember who we believe in and trust.

Royalty runs in our veins! We have a right to sit in heavily places with You! We are sons and daughters of the Most High God! All that belongs to You is available to me as well. If we walk upright before You, Your Word says You will withhold no good thing from us! Our blessings are earmarked for us and we have privileges from our King!

Wherever I go, I represent kingdom. Whatever my feet tread upon… that shall You give me. I dwell in the place called Bethel; for that is where You reside. Beckon us and challenge us to come up higher to gain knowledge from Your throne room. Sing a new song over us, oh God! All things are at Your command, and even the enemy can't make a move on us unless You allow it! We vow to use any and all test for growth and development for the kingdom.

Father, we realize that tribulation was never meant to destroy us. We are learning that tribulation teaches us patience in a way that seems unjust to the natural eye. Tribulation occurs in order for kingdoms to grow battles that are won around us. Settle us, visit us, and keep us in this hour. We desire more than just church; we desire You, oh King. We know You by name:

-Ruler of the entire universe
-Everlasting Father
-Breasted One
-Omniscient (All knowing)
-Omnipotent (All powerful)

-Omnipresent (Everywhere)
-Light Giver
-Comforter
-Oxygen Creator
-The One who formed us from the foundation of the world
-Our Great and Mighty King
-Giver and Sustainer of Life
-He who upholds the elements of the world simply by His Word
-The One who trampled over the enemy when His children call
-The One who brags on us and says consider them for they will never fail Me

    Thank You God for loving us beyond who we are and blessing us with all things pertaining to Your kingdom! Establish it today and seal it forever! Amen and amen!"

Trust Your Journey - Share Your Thoughts

Trust Your Journey - Share Your Thoughts

Supplication

"God, You said the king's heart is in Your hand and You turn it in whatever direction You choose. It pleases You to bless Your children with miracles, signs and wonders. You give us our heart's desires when we diligently seek You, to include financial blessings and employment. Bless those who are struggling and without a job to receive work that they know in their heart could only come from You. Allow every application to be approved at Your will, even those that may not have enough education, or academically qualified.

You have already commanded the blessing over their job, home and family! They put their trust in You of God! You have children that are financial givers and ready to give to the Kingdom upon job approval! Honor them with employment so they can give what is purposed in their heart to do.

God, You are calling Your people to draw even closer to You! Stir up the gifts You have placed in them. This is the hour that will be a witness and testimony to others. Thank You for blessing Your children that have a heart to serve You unconditionally. Lord, I thank You now for spreading Your favor to those in need of employment! In Jesus Name, amen and amen!"

Trust Your Journey - Share Your Thoughts

Surrender

"Father You are sovereign. You are the very air I breathe. I was created to live in Your presence. There is no life apart from You. Today, I surrender all to You for every part of me belongs to You. I withhold nothing from You and bow at Your feet, most Holy King. You come swiftly and I yield to Your invasion. Come, Holy Spirit and do as You desire. I give all of me away to be in Your presence so You can use me. As my ear continues to listen to Your voice, I desire that You speak and move in whatever way You choose.

Invade us oh God! Invade us and allow our mind to become Yours. Most Holy One, we yield to You on this day. The harvest is ready for picking and You need laborers to gather what you've prepared. We want to be children of obedience in this hour.

When You walk in, all negativity in our lives must disappear! All we want is You; not the blessing, but Your presence! When we receive You, all else will follow. We're hungry, thirsty and desperate for You. The only thing that will satisfy our thirst is an encounter with You!"

Trust Your Journey - Share Your Thoughts

Deeper

"Father, You stated in Your word that those who hunger and thirst for righteous shall be filled. God, we hunger for You today. When Your children become hungry, You will not deny them, for You do not want them to die of thirst! As the deer desperately pants for the water, so does our soul long for You. Lord in this hour, we do not want to be a professional Christian, but we want to be Christians that are increasingly desperate for You!

God visit us like never before and create such an awaking within us that it causes us to die to self! When You come and invade us, we must die to our flesh daily as we live in Your presence. Kill our flesh Lord and let us crucify all things that displease You! Flesh, we command You to yield to the Holy Spirit today and walk in obedience to His plans and purposes for our lives. Father, we are Your children and we desire to become more and more like You each day, hour and minute! We need the blessing of hunger and thirsting after You! Feed us Lord, feed us!"

Trust Your Journey - Share Your Thoughts

Confidence

"Father, Your promises to us are yes and amen. You said in Your Word that You will supply all our needs according to Your riches in glory. You know what we have need of before we ask. We come today standing on Your promises that are found in Your Word. You are not only a loving God but You are also a jealous God; no other Gods shall come before You. Teach us to war for what is right as the enemy desires to sift us like wheat. His plans for us are imperfect; Your plans are matchless. You desire for us to be hidden under Your shadow.

Jesus Christ sits at Your right hand. You want us to seek those things above, and not things on this earth that will divide and conquer us. Create in us a clean heart and renew the right spirit within us. Yes Lord, we submit to You today and we desire nothing more than to please You. The first step to pleasing You is obeying You in all things. Thank You for allowing our steps to be ordered by You, and for making our crooked places straight."

Trust Your Journey - Share Your Thoughts

Adoration

"Daddy, we praise and adore You; for this is the day You created. Father, the trees have spoken this morning and they praise You with their substance. The bird awakens and praises You with their song. The sun awakens and praises You with its light. As Your people awaken this morning, allow them to praise You with their hearts. You said in Your Word to let everything that has breath praise You! Psalms 150:6 Let everything that has breath praise Adonai!"

Trust Your Journey - Share Your Thoughts

Revelation

"Lord, we are open to receive truth and revelation from You this morning in whatever form You want to send it. We may not always understand how You move, how Your choices or decisions were made, and the way you execute them. But we forever call You Faithful to us as our Way Maker, Sustainer, and Redeemer. When all things around us fail, You remain faithful to us.

Thank You for granting us access to who You are and what You desire. We are Your people and citizens of Your kingdom. You have commanded the blessings upon Your people and have also commanded suffering. We can't have one without the other. Our mind, will and emotions cry out for a deeper walk and experience with You. We request that You grant us access this morning as we honor You. Come Holy Spirit, rest and abide in us. You have permission today to overtake us with Your goodness!"

Trust Your Journey - Share Your Thoughts

Invitation

"Father, we petition You this morning to hover over us. Make us sensitive to Your presence as You walk in a room; no matter where that room is. Let us be mindful of Your anointing upon our lives. Wherever we are, You are as well! Come, Holy Spirit come. Arrest us, chase us and captivate us! Sing over us, dance with us and speak life in us as we speak to You! Good morning:

-Daddy
-Adonai
-King
-Savior
-One who lifts our heads
-Redeemer
-Healer
-Burden Bearer
-Financial Planner
-Contract Sustainer
-Life Giver
-Visionary
-Curse Breaker
-Provider
-Banner
-Most High God

Good morning!"

Trust Your Journey - Share Your Thoughts

Sustainability

"Father, thank You for giving us all things pertaining to life and Godliness. Please don't allow us to become weary in well doing; for in due season, we shall reap if we faint not. You are so faithful to us and we so appreciate Your Holy Spirit guiding our footsteps. We are seated in heavenly places, and You delight in blessing Your people.

God, as our hands war for the promises, let us be mindful that we also need a time to rest, regroup, and re-strategize on what You want us to do next. We call you the Strategic Thinker and You have equipped us to be strategic with a winning blueprint! The enemy has gone back to his drawing board, and he is trying to come up with another way to beat us!

Lord, You said greater that You are in us than he that is in the world! You also stated that no weapon formed against us shall prosper! You prepare a table for us in the presence of our enemies. Thank You for Your light shining bright upon us. We are the light of the world and the salt of the earth. Increase is given to us wherever we go, and every place our feet tread, You have given to us as well! We command the blessings and they come forth. Thank You for favor and for putting us on the minds and hearts of people to sow seeds of blessing to us! Amen!"

Trust Your Journey - Share Your Thoughts

Intercession for Leadership

"Father we intercede on behalf of Pastor's and their leadership teams all over this nation. God You have called us to be midwives for those that we minister to. We don't take this call lightly, and we recognize that our assignment is not always valued or appreciated. Yet, we stand knowing that we can't come off the wall; for this has been our purpose from the foundation of the world. You snatched us out and gave us unique purpose to lead people to You.

Contrary to popular belief, Daddy we do not want the glory; however, we want people to grow and glorify You! We do not want to be placed on a pedestal as if we can't be broken. You know all the weight we carry, and the things that keep us up at night and calling Your name. We become counselors for couples seeking divorce, for those who want to live ungodly, and for members who can't and/or refuse to reach their full potential. We have this assignment for our children who go astray at times, and we offer our love and support for our spouses who carry the load with us.

Daddy in this hour You are so hungry for us to remain faithful and cry out to You like never before! As we stand in the gap, we see that we can't go back if we wanted to. We can't go back to the past, to the mundane and fearful ways of living. Our 'yes' to You delivers someone out of bondage and causes them to change their mind!

As a collective body, we are asking and seeking an intercession on our behalf, and of those around us. We stand in the gap today taking hits as good soldiers; knowing that our reward is nigh. We will not faint, but be of good courage and wait on You!

Tonight, we ask you to restore us dear God and Creator of all things. As we rest, let us not forget how blessed we are to have You in our lives. Thank You for providing us with people You have tasked to assist those who would have suffered in silence. We want Your fullness God, not the spirit of depression or suicide to infiltrate our homes, churches, children, or us!

Our commitment as a team is to restore and care for one another as You have for us. We are devoted to holding up the arms of our Apostle and Pastors, and to care for them so they do not fall prey to the enemy.

Forgive us Father for not caring for the shepherd as we should. Help us to never forget how important it is to respect, appreciate and cover leadership. Thank You for reminding us to care! Amen!"

Trust Your Journey - Share Your Thoughts

Trust Your Journey - Share Your Thoughts

Persecution

"Father what path do I take when those close to me are the ones who persecute me? Where do I turn when every fiery dart is coming toward me? Who do I ask for help when the ones You think You can count on are the ones smearing Your name and reputation? Today as I fast, I turn to the Rock, the One that is higher than I. You are my Shield, my Banner and the One who lifts my head. Those in my very midst want to see me fail. I curse every spoken word against Your anointed servant. Let every unjust word wrestle with those who have spoken against me. I am Your servant and give love freely even when it is not returned to me.

Judge Your people today oh God, when people want to be around me for the wrong motives, steal from me and judge me. Let them know that the loneliness, hurt, financial struggles, and depression are all portals that have been opened because they put their mouth on Your daughter. They are hound dogs and bark to alert those around them, that they have found their prey. Set a trap for them. They say they love You, yet they try Your anointed. Their words reflect that they are going to heaven, yet they listen to slander. They claim to have my back, yet they open their ear gates to sit with those who persecute me. Cause disruption today and let them know that it is because of what they did, saw, and heard.

I thank You for showing me who is really for me and who is using me. I thank You for telling me to guard up and move out. I'm grateful that You have hidden me and all those that I desire to carry with me, cannot go. I release them today and I say send in new hearts and new vision carriers.

Send in the saints who will uplift my arms and not drop me. Send in those who will understand my passion and carry out the vision. I need women of God who will lift me daily in prayer and ward off each trap that has been set for me. Send in those who will support financially without hesitation or question. This is my prayer today. "But You, O Lord, are a shield about me, my glory, and the lifter of my head." Psalms 3:3 ESV"

Trust Your Journey - Share Your Thoughts

Petition

"Father we need You to move today. Move in our marriages, homes, and our situations. Move on our behalf Lord. We can't stomach the fact that others seem to be blessed yet, we Your people sit in total barrenness simply for obeying Your voice. How long shall the righteous be left in isolation? How long before You curse that which has attempted to curse us? There is a war that goes on in our members that causes us to doubt our stand and position in You.

We hope, yet we are torn.
We press, yet we are challenged.
We cry, yet we rejoice.
We need doors to open and change to come.
We need debts cancelled and burdens removed.
We need vision to come to pass and that it only happens in Your presence.

We are tired of being spiritually schizophrenic, and we're exhausted of being unsure and unstable in our thought process. Who can we turn to Daddy, and who can we run to? The only place and person we can run to is You; for You are higher than we are. Please don't allow the ungodly heathen to continue to wage war against Your people. Let the redeemed say so! Help us find comfort and safety in You.

Lord, we are Your people, a royal priesthood and a peculiar nation. We shall show forth Your praise and we shall not be ashamed to press and call upon Your name. Who are You that we are mindful of You? You are the Most High God! You are the Repairer of the breach and we need every breach to be repaired.

Every stone You want removed must be destroyed, and every cursed eliminated! Your will must be done in us and on earth, as it is in heaven. How long before You come Daddy and how much longer shall we tarry? Open the floodgates and make all things clear to us! Open the doors for us! Cause the attacks to cease for a season so we can gain access and strength in You. Hold us up when we are weak and comfort us when we need it.

Father, challenge us and move in us like never before. This is our prayer to You today, Holy One. Let Your glory rise in us and Your Word become more prevalent than the attacks; for Your Word is a lamp unto our feet and a light unto our path. Most Holy One, provide assurance and restoration for Your people today. Holy Spirit, cause chains to break, and release a charge over Your angels on our behalf. Lord, let peace arise all around us; cause Your face to shine. Most Holy One, come! Come in the midst of where we are and what we say and do. Speak a right now Word that will transform the space we stand, work, sleep, and walk in!"

Trust Your Journey - Share Your Thoughts

Trust Your Journey - Share Your Thoughts

Exchange

"Lord God, we await Your arrival and anticipate what You want to say to us. We know the following practices are NOT the answer to any challenges: Isolation, anger, unforgiveness, gossip and slander, fornication, adultery, lies, running away from responsibilities, drinking and shutting down our feelings.

The following responses are true answers to our concerns: You, oh God are the true answer to our trials and tests. We seek You and cast all our cares upon You. Lord, show us the way to be still, listen, cry out, and make our request known; while we seek and run to You in our time of need. Our answer includes love, joy, peace, and confessing one to another that we may be healed. We must bow before our King and make a joyful noise, while we humble ourselves.

We exchange our ways of thinking to Yours, Daddy. Make a deposit in us so we can make a withdrawal from You. Give us the exchange so we can see clearly. Cause Your face to shine upon us and we shall be healed. Exchange is paramount in this hour, so we make it and take it today. My thoughts are not Your thoughts, and my ways are not Your ways… exchange them today.

Cast who I think I am as far as the east is from the west. I fling myself upon You today oh God, and I ask You to transform the inner man to please You. There is a war going on in our churches and if we are going to win, we must know when to address it and when to retreat. Teach our hands to war and our mouths to speak Your word. In Jesus Name, Amen."

Trust Your Journey - Share Your Thoughts

Intercession for Prayer Warriors

"Father, I pray for the intercessors this morning. Help them to not miss their assignment to pray for others. As they walk through their own personal issues, financial and friendship matters, spousal concerns, work and self-issues; increase their prayer responsibilities. Lord, You are speaking to Senior Leaders as well as Executive Teams concerning where we are as a church. We are sending out mandates that midwives must birth in this season.

Jesus, call Your intercessors unto You. Call them into Your throne room so they can really see the enemy's plot that has been laid out against the church. Allow them in, so they will know that You will also hold them accountable. Their accountability is affected when they choose not to respond, speak up, or stay on the wall as You have instructed.

Lord, take the gloves off and rebuke, chastise, correct, and comfort these Your servants until they look, smell, speak, and move like You. Teach their mouths to war and not their emotions. Take them into the third heaven so You can show them things in the spirit. Father arrest them through Your visitation with them. Lord, become relentless in Your pursuit after them.

You are trying to birth a spiritual baby! Midwives are needed to get in position so we can push without ripping or tearing an area that will cause damage! Father, we want to birth but we have no midwives consistently in place to push. Father, my spirit grieves for them today. Speak to them today! Wherever they are in their walk, speak! Convict and deal with them in a manner that will cause them to run to You with a new pace! This is my prayer, amen."

Trust Your Journey - Share Your Thoughts

Presence

"Our affection and devotion is poured out on the heart of Jesus. Father, I adore You for Your lovingkindness and tender mercies. Great is Your faithfulness! Father, thank You for revelation and wisdom in knowing You are good, and You are God. It's not wrapped up in who we think we are, but who You created us to be. From the foundation of the world, You created us to be whole and complete in You. Your presence surrounds us even when we may not always acknowledge it. Lord, Your presence is hovering over us and we yield to this moment so You can come in.

Invade us with Your presence and capture us with Your undying love. Our hearts cry out for the true and living God. We are thirsty only for You! Capture us oh God, and move us from barrenness to fullness of joy. Your love is never ending, and if we had ten thousand tongues, we still could not express just how great You are. Draw us into Your bosom Lord, and nourish us like only You can.

I pray Daddy that You will invade our lives, homes, bank accounts, marriages, and our demeanor. Let us reflect Your image and grace. We comprehend that it is not by our might, or by our power, but by Your spirit that we exist! Give us wisdom, and allow the eyes of our understanding to be enlightened, so we may understand the call You have placed on us!

Thank You for touching our minds and revealing things You want us to be freed from. As Your servants rest and before they rise, I pray supernatural strength shall be deposited into them, in the name of Jesus! May the day be great, the morning shine forth, and may our voice awaken to give You praise! Amen!"

Trust Your Journey - Share Your Thoughts

Desire

"Jesus, order our steps today. Teach us to drink from Your well that never runs dry. Quench our thirst for You. We are dry and parched, so we come to the well! Fill us up with all the fullness of who You are. Lord, You are the Living Water and the Bread of Life. You are the sponge we absorb and the one who satisfies our lack. Remind us that You have not left us, but are seeking those who thirst for you. God, we desire more and more of You. Come today and answer all things. Provide deliverance in areas where we need deliverance. Come into our homes and our churches to set people free. Don't leave us where we started, but move us into perfection.

Our declaration will be to run to our thirst quencher and bow before the One who feeds us! We rejoice today knowing who we belong to. We declare that the heavens and flood gates remain open, and a fresh revelation be provided. Soldiers will rise for Your kingdom and will tarry until we receive power from on high. Your power will come upon us like a blanket to warm the atmosphere and release signs and wonders upon Your people! We thank You God for those moments, in Jesus Name, amen!"

Trust Your Journey - Share Your Thoughts

Breakthrough

"Lord, I pray churches everywhere will explode with Your presence and divine visitations. May saints come forth requesting walls be broken. I pray every angel assigned to our churches will be on post today! May financial resources saturate our ministries! I pray every soul connected to our ministries is drawn to Your anointing!

Father, allow Your Holy Spirit to move on us and take us to places we have never been. Catapult us into a new realm and seal it so no demon or devil can break through. Your presence is all we desire, and Your Word is what we need. It is in Jesus that we live, move and have our very being. BE who You are in us today! Meet every need spiritually, financially, emotionally and socially as You care about our concerns! You have already given us all things pertaining to life and Godliness, and we rejoice in You, oh Great King! Amen!"

Trust Your Journey - Share Your Thoughts

Cleansing

"Jesus, I thank You this morning and marvel at the glory that resides in Your house. I pray Daddy, that the lethargic spirit that attempts to capture the hearts and minds of the people will be bound today. Father, You prophetically spoke to our house that the old things must go so the new can rush in with vision.

Lord, send in a fresh movement of Your guidance and remove all decisions that displease You at our church. If it is negative opinions, remove them. If it's slandered word curses, get rid of it. It is time for the people to leave who bring accusations or speak against Your man and woman of God. We surrender to Your will and Your purpose for us today.

God, have Your way as You shift the atmosphere and Your people. Let the redeemed of the Lord walk in victory and let the anointed soldiers rise in this hour. Expose to us where the tricks and breaches are so we can march forward in victory. You are faithful and we want to honor You with a clean house. As You enter into our thoughts, let our minds be on You and You alone. It's time to honor You for who You are. Thank You Jesus for Your presence and Your Word that will bring even more deliverance to our church today! Send it Lord, send it!"

Trust Your Journey - Share Your Thoughts

Faith

"Father, we adore Your presence that is forever surrounding us. Your peace and comfort are near. You are altogether lovely and we call You Beautiful. We kiss Your face today, honor Your glory upon us, and all You have entrusted to us. You are Devine and Holy, and encamp around those who fear You, but also love You. Be our portion today, Oh God. You desire all of who we are in You, so our cup can run over! Lord, we desire daily encounters with You as You speak to us in dreams and visions.

We are fully aware that You are well able to rescue us from all fiery darts. We want to see things in the Spirit and not in the natural, and we want to gaze from Your perspective and not ours God. Thank You for causing our character to line up with the promise. We are grateful for testing our hearts to see if our life is about us, or about You and Your will for the kingdom. We wait in confident expectation for what You are going to do during an open heaven season. We need our portion and our share of the promise because we have been faithful and obedient. You declared for us to eat the good of the land!

Oh Trusted One, thank You for being our accountability partner. You know what we do, say and think. Your Spirit is here and holding us accountable for our actions. You know everything we have lost and all that we shall gain. Send Your mighty army to ride with us, war with us, sustain us, speak Your truth to us, and strengthen us! Be our portion, Jesus. May Your time of correcting, chastening, and punishing us be lessened.

Bless us with new mercies, God; for You said in Your Word that it shall follow us all the days of our lives. We accept our portion from the kingdom. Your desire for our lives is to be complete according to Proverbs 4:23-27. We must be diligent in our pursuit of You. Bless us to settle ourselves, set goals, and expect results. We declare today that we will walk in victory. Portals remain open so we can capture Your blessings in the spirit as they manifest in the natural. We are opened to hear your voice clearly.

Daddy, we kiss Your face today and keep our ears nailed to the doorpost of Your heart! Thank You for the new year of birthing! It is important to You in this season that we do not abort or kill the spiritual baby you have charged us to keep healthy until the day of delivery. We surrender to the birthing process today, Lord. We say send the midwives to coach us, encourage us and to tell us when to push out this baby.

Midwives arise and take Your place as you move into your assignment. We push today Father, for the labor has been intense! We are ready to deliver Your spiritual blessing! When we look upon it, we will forget the process of trials and tests, and concentrate on the gift. Father, we want You to breathe in and through us, and thank You once again for being our portion. Lamentations 3:24 KJV "The LORD is my portion," says my soul, "therefore I will hope in him.""

Trust Your Journey - Share Your Thoughts

Trust Your Journey - Share Your Thoughts

Exhortation

"Great King, we adore You today. My heart and my tongue is like a pen of a ready scribe; excited to explore Your beauty and splendor, as I cast and fling myself upon You. Who can know Your beauty except those that fear You? Lord, who can understand Your plans except those that seek You? We can't stay where we are; we must move into our next.

We love You Father, for Your arrows are sharp in the heart of our enemies. We stay under the shadow of Your wings, so we are not destroyed. There are many that seek to disrupt Your plans and purposes for our lives, but we surrender only to King Jesus. Lord, we speak Your oracles over ourselves to allow the Holy Spirit to come and overtake us.

Saturate us with Your ever-present love, God. No man can ever duplicate the height, depth and width of Your love for Your people. Your mercies are new daily, and today, they cause us to blow You a kiss, for You have heard our cry. Your mercies are near; for we have turned from our wicked ways.

Oh Daddy, You have blanketed us with Your peace. Even when we suffer for Your sake, we will be mindful of Your promises. Thank You for carrying us through each storm and for being closer than the very breath we breathe. Thank You for drawing nigh unto us, and for Your healing and resurrection power.

God, we shout from the depths of our soul that we love You Lord! What we can't utter, we write with our hearts. What is unexplainable becomes tangible in Your presence. Oh, taste and see that You are good to us! We are blessed and highly favored when we obey Your Word.

Thank You, Lord for the blood of Jesus that continues to cleanse us from all unrighteousness. God, thank You for Your sanctifying power through Your Word that washes us. We belong to You; as citizens of Your kingdom, we walk in the sonship of our King. You said greater works shall we do, and we want the greater to follow us. Master, we cling to Your heart and bow in Your throne room as we wait with anticipation of Your arrival.

Lord, we have entered Your gates with thanksgiving and Your courts with praise. God, we are so thankful unto You and bless Your Holy Name. As we bow, You enter and take Your seat on the throne as Your angels begin to sing over us. God, You open the scroll and see our names written in it. Jesus, You release us to worship, and impart wisdom. Lord, You send forth the promises, sing over us, hold us and transform our minds. Nothing feels more real than bowing before You. Take this clay that we call "us" and shape us today. Remind us that we are frail and only become whole in Your presence. We fall under Your command, in Jesus Name!"

Trust Your Journey - Share Your Thoughts

Trust Your Journey - Share Your Thoughts

Expectation

"Daddy, this morning I rejoice in knowing that I will see You again. My bones and skin ache for Your presence. I want to wrap myself up into who You are. Lord, I desire to know You and the power of Your resurrection. You are my portion; therefore, I hope in You. My flesh longs and hungers for the true and living God.

Speak to my essence King Jesus. Speak to those parts of me that don't see, know or understand my purpose. Speak to those areas that need re-birthing and clarity. Arise in us oh God like never before. Make Your face to shine upon us so we can be well! Walk with us through each day and through each emotion we experience in You. We love to walk with You, Jesus during times of joy, peace, and even when we stumble and fall.

Lord, there is no door that You will not kick open for us! There is no windowpane You will not break to reach us, and no storm is hard for you to maneuver to rescue us! God, You will run to the uttermost parts of the earth to cover and shield us from unseen danger! Lord, You are strong and mighty, and mighty in battle. You are not coming after us to punish, but to vindicate us! Jesus, You are the rescinder of floods, forces of nature, and our wind. You are the sun and rain! Pour over us and don't hold back your rain.

God, the very elements of Your power are now awakening because they don't know how to hold back Your presence. The mountains shake and the skies release Your spirit as they rejoice that You are near. Every element on earth will experience the fact that You are coming! We are seated and locked in with spiritual seatbelts so we can be ready for the ride!

Lord, we see Your mighty army in formation, and we know that You have placed Your sword in their hands. You are coming after us to birth revival as we yield to the birthing today. God, we take a deep breath and breathe in Your anointing and Your Word this morning. Oh, that men would praise You for Your marvelous works! Amen! Psalms 40:6."

Trust Your Journey - Share Your Thoughts

Awakening

"Father, this is the hour You are awakening Your children from our sleep. You awaken us with pain and suffering, and with trials and persecution. It is written in Your word that those who live Godly will suffer persecution; there is no way around this truth. What You desire from us is to continue to have faith as a mustard seed and remove any negative doubt from our lives. We must remember in this hour that You do not withhold Your promises; for Your Word never lies.

Help us remember God, that all things work together for our good. We are the royal priesthood, and citizens that You have given authority to police up our churches and homes. We are not only heirs but joint heirs with You who is seated in heavenly places. Whatsoever we speak and have faith to believe in You, will be done!

God, Your world needs You! Our cities, workplaces, children, family members, and homes need You! Visit Your people where they are and whatever state they're in. Your arm is not short that You can't reach us! You are Omniscient (all knowing), Omnipotent (all powerful), and Omnipresent (You are everywhere). No other god can claim that title.

Lord, You are simultaneous and feed all of us at the same time. All we need to do is come and dine with You, and You will make all things good in its time. Fill us God until we are full, not with ourselves but with You! Fill us God so we can win many for Your kingdom, and empty us so we don't think we are the kingdom. Break in God and break us, cleanse us, and speak to us!

Jesus, kick down the doors and walls that we place around ourselves. When we attempt to safeguard ourselves, we're really shutting You out, and those You have placed in our lives! Daddy shift situations, circumstances and people around us. Place us strategically in Your kingdom to make the next move. We long to hear You say, "Well done my good and faithful servant."

Lies must cease concerning us! Deception must be exposed around us! Sickness and disease must bow down to Your voice around us! Financial breakthroughs must support Your cause for the kingdom. Lord, realignment is knocking at our doors, and we open it with great anticipation and expectation! Great King, You are about to make us laugh.

    Oh God, align Your people once again. You are shifting in the earth and summoning Your people to come hear what Your next move is. Lord, You are calling many from every corner of the earth. Thank You Jesus for loving us, forgiving us and never giving up on us!"

Trust Your Journey - Share Your Thoughts

Trust Your Journey - Share Your Thoughts

Obedience

"Adonai and Lover of my soul, thank You for caring about us and loving us beyond what You see. Your love for us surpasses our own understanding. Lord, Your desire to commune with us is the fire that consumes You for eternity. You hunger for Your chosen citizens and committed to us for life. You don't quit on us when we mess up, or walk out the door when we don't please You. You never wish ill-will on us when we fall.

Jesus, You always show faithful love through action and deed! God, You are serious about binding us to You, and You chase hard after us. No matter where we are or what we do, Your love chases us down. Your Word said if I make my bed in hell, You are there. There is no place I can run to that You are not present! You are:

-Faithful
-Consistent
-Merciful
-Kind
-Relentless
-Constant Pursuer
-Unrestrained
-Ferocious

Lord, all You ask is that we come to You, incline our ears, hear what You've spoken to us, and walk in obedience to the instructions your share from Your throne room. Daddy, our heart's desire today is to be conformed into the imagine of Your dear Son, Jesus! Create in us a clean heart and renew the right spirit within us!

Jesus, pour out fresh revelation and knowledge regarding Your direction and purpose for us. We want a manifestation with results from You, as we cling to the purpose that is birthed in this hour. Bless us with the promises You have for us, oh God; we have pursued them with passion!

Father, You are King and Lord; apart from You, there is no other. Come swiftly to meet us exactly where we are. God, remove burdens, make instructions clear, and order our steps in You. Please don't let us run after our own devises but let us yield to Your will. According to Psalms 13, how long will You hide Your face and Your promises from us! Don't allow the enemy to have the upper hand on us God; help us to keep going and bring delight to our souls.

Lord, we will rejoice in You and tell of Your goodness. This is the year of promises, and Your people desire it to come to pass. Pick us up God, so our souls can delight in Your goodness. Remember Your covenant with Your children and move on our behalf. We desire to please only You and not our flesh! We are excited to see people transformed and renewed. Move on our behalf Father, in Jesus Name, amen!"

Trust Your Journey - Share Your Thoughts

Trust Your Journey - Share Your Thoughts

Deliverance

"Father, pressure is all around me but I will not surrender to it. When I want to run and give up, I'm reminded through Your Word how much You love me. God, You sent Your Son to die on the cross for my sins while He was without sin. Each week I battle in my mind about what direction to go in and what road to take; each week You keep me going.

Lord, I will fail if You are not with me. Please allow Your blood to cover, cleanse, and restore what has died. If a witch is in my midst, destroy her! If a non-giver is in my midst, dismiss them! If anyone is around me who is not faithful, remove them. I need You Lord and You are the only road map I can take. You are the only Storm Chaser, Burden Remover, and Way Maker. I need You Lord as my heart, mind and will aches for You to deliver me. Bring Your deliverance back to me, oh God! I need Your glory back into my life! Please show me the way!

I wait patiently for my King to deliver me. For they that wait upon the Lord shall renew their strength, they shall mount up with wings as eagles; they shall run and not be weary, they shall walk and not faint. Daddy, I wait upon You today to bring me out. I can no longer do it in my own strength, so exchange my strength with whatever You desire to give me.

Come, oh God like a mighty rushing wind to every situation. Forgive me of my shortcomings and ways that did not please You. Jesus, all I desire today is Your will. All of my righteousness is nothing but a filthy rag in Your sight. I submit and humble myself under You Mighty God, so You can be exalted. You are the only true and Living God, and my life belongs to You.

Daddy, avenge every attack and trap that has been set. When You deliver me, I will shout it from the mountain tops and proclaim it wherever I go. I shall shout that my God is the Deliverer who still performs miracles, and has never forsaken His people. Thank You Lord for Your mercy, and thank You for Your roots that are deep within me! I surrender God!"

Trust Your Journey - Share Your Thoughts

Increase

"Father, thank You for this day, and for Your mercy that endures forever. I thank You for the commitment of Your Word which you promised to us for life. We praise You Lord, as You dwell in our hearts so we can be rooted and grounded in Your love. We know it is Your desire for us to seek the highest good for others without motive for personal gain. We bless You Father, and take comfort in knowing that You have the vision of what we shall become.

Daddy, we want to catch hold of Your divine substance, so we won't have plastic faith, but a faith that is rooted in You and Your Word. We want to be planted where we can grow to obtain all the nutrients we need to do Your will. Teach us Lord to push past our promises, nurture it, and cherish it eternally. Give us wisdom on how to conduct all of our affairs in You. We yield to You Jesus, so You can increase in us. Amen!"

Trust Your Journey - Share Your Thoughts

Lovingkindness

"Father, I applaud You this morning for affording me the privilege to wake up and clothed in my right mind. I am grateful for the activity of my limbs, and a willing heart to hear You speak to me this morning. Father, we are Judah, Your chosen people.

You are a big-hearted God who desires for our hearts to be enormous as well. God, You are engaged in doing good for Your people. Thank You for allowing us to feel Your love and peace today. Allow Your big heart to manifest in those that love and need You. Pour out Your Holy Spirit and dispatch Your angels, Lord. Place them on assignment in our homes, jobs, finances, and in our dealings with others.

God, as we lay our head to rest under Your wings tonight, let us be mindful that we rest because of You. Let us remember that we will open our eyes in the morning because of You. Your mercy endures with us forever, and You have been faithful to us daily; even if the circumstances are favorable or unfavorable.

Lord, we still believe with full understanding that all things work for our good. Give us dreams, visions and revelation as You continue to comfort us. Lord, allow all of our children, spouses and family members to rest tonight. Mighty One, give Your angels charge over us, and cover us from the snares of the enemy. In Jesus Name, amen!"

Trust Your Journey - Share Your Thoughts

www.ingramcontent.com/pod-product-compliance
Lightning Source LLC
Chambersburg PA
CBHW072028110526
44592CB00012B/1425